Follow

CW00690291

"The highest expression of Humankind is the full engagement and joy that allows us to evolve by learning from and leaving the past behind, by consciously and consistently expressing our authentic potential and making our unique contribution to the world, taking our direction from Spirit, being physically vital, having all the resources we need to fulfill our destiny and taking actions that are only for the greater good of the world. In other words, we're designed to feel good being who we are and doing what we came here to do." - Karen Curry Parker

Introduction to Quantum Human Design

An Imprint for GracePoint Publishing (www.GracePointPublishing.com)
GracePoint Matrix, LLC
322 N Tejon St. #207
Colorado Springs CO 80903
www.GracePointMatrix.com

Email: Admin@GracePointMatrix.com

SAN # 991-6032

Library of Congress Control Number:	2020950175
ISBN-13: (Paperback)	978-1-951694-17-3
ISBN Ebook	978-1-951694-18-0
ISBN: Paperback Color:	978-1-951694-24-1
ISBN": Ebook Color:	978-1-951694-29-6

Compiled and Created by, Kristin Anne
https://www.instagram.com/kria.madetolove/

Contents

WHAT IS QUANTUM HUMAN DESIGN?

Quantum Human Design is often called the "new Astrology," and the "intersection of science and spirituality." Your Quantum Human Design chart is formulated by taking your birth date, time, and location – giving you specific information about your life path, your style of working, your relationship blueprint, how you experience energy in the world, and most importantly, how to create a truly meaningful and authentic life.

Quantum Human Design is a synthesis of Eastern and Western Astrology, the Chinese, I'Ching, The Kabbalah, the Hindu Chakra System and Quantum Physics. Your Human Design chart is calculated using your birth date, time and place.

If you're like most of our clients, you've probably attended multiple personal growth seminars and read lots of books about manifesting "change" and creating success in your life. Maybe you've even studied specific techniques to help you release "blocks" and get yourself "unstuck".

But you still haven't seen the results you've been hoping for. (Even though you've been doing everything "right.") It's not your fault.

The single most important reason you may have not had the success you've been working so hard for is this:

A One Size Fits All Approach to Life Does NOT Work!

All people are equally valuable and important. AND each of us has our own energetic blueprint and individual style of operating successfully in life. What might work for one person doesn't necessarily work for another.

A Human Design chart offers an astonishingly accurate guide to your personality, as well as direction and guidance on how you can deal with challenges in your life. It also shows you your personal "formula" for creating what you want in your life.

Previously, Human Design charts have been notoriously difficult to interpret and decipher – until now. Quantum Human Design, a modern way of interpreting Human Design, offers you an incredibly down-to-earth, practical way to understand your Human Design chart.

Quantum Human Design Specialists are highly trained coaches, mentors and guides who have learned a way of interpreting your chart that is simple, easy to follow, clear, and gives you solid, workable strategies to help you discover exactly what you need to do to bring out the best of who you are in your life.

Learning your Human Design:

☑ Confirms what you already know, sense or have felt about yourself.

☑ Gives you full permission and confidence to really step fully into your Truth.

☑ Confirms the themes you may have noticed playing out in your life & relationships.

☑ Gives you deeper understanding to why you are the way you are & feel the way you do.

☑ Enables you to not take things personally because you realize everything is just energy.

☑ Deepens your compassion, patience and ultimately love for yourself and others.

Think of it this way:

Human Design is a synthesis of ancient wisdom and modern science. It is a collection of all the potential archetypes located in a single "map." That map not only tells you where you would feel good and helps you navigate a path to get there, it also gives you a new way of thinking about who you really are.

Quantum Human Design teaches you to look at your Human Design Chart (your personal "map") as a story. Over the course of your life you've been told a story of who you are. Maybe that story led down a career path that isn't really making your soul soar. Maybe your story has you living out patterns that keep you from believing you can have what you really want in your life. Maybe the story you've been trying to keep up with all your life isn't even really your story.

Quantum Human Design will give you the words – the story – of Who You Truly Are.

If you're going to create an authentic life – a life that is yours – you've got to start with knowing Who You Are and what you need to do to get started living the story you were born to live.

Your personal Quantum Human Design Chart can reveal your strengths, your weaknesses, and perhaps most importantly, your potential. Prepare for repetitive difficulties that you might encounter throughout your life, and embrace the opportunity to grow as you understand your personal Human Design strategy.

You'll discover your path to living an aligned, authentic, vital and truly meaningful life simply by following the directions set out in your Human Design chart – the "owner's manual" to your life.

THE HUMAN DESIGN CHART

"Your Human Design is your key to understanding your energy, your Life Purpose, your Life Path and your Soul's journey in this lifetime. You are a once-in-a-lifetime cosmic event and the fulfillment of your potential and purpose is the greatest gift you can give the world." - Karen Curry Parker

Get your free Human Design Chart (https://freehumandesignchart.com/)

YOUR QUANTUM BLUEPRINT

The moment of your conception marked an important, once-in-a-lifetime event. At that moment the Universe joined your Soul with a powerful story, the story of your life. The story of You is so unique that it has never been on the planet before and will never be on the planet again.

Over the course of your life, you may have forgotten your story. You may have been told that you "should" be a certain way, act a certain way and that there are key formulas that you have to follow to be successful or healthy.

If you're like most people, you may have struggled to make the rules you were given fit or work for you. You may have followed the rules very well and still not gotten the results for which you were hoping. Your journey may have left you feeling depleted and not good enough. You may have lost touch with the powerful story of Who You Truly Are and felt that there is something wrong with you.

There is nothing wrong with you! You just need to remember Who You Truly Are!

It makes sense that if you are a once-in-a-lifetime event in this Universe that there are no "formulas" for health and vitality, abundance, right relationship, right work, or success in life other than the ones that work for you.

There is no one-size-fits-all approach to creating success. In fact, even the definition of success is unique to each one of us. The greatest source of pain in life is the disconnect from our Authentic Self—the real story of Who You Truly Are.

When we try to squeeze the powerful essence of Who We Are behind masks or into small definitions of who we should be, it unleashes a subtle restlessness inside of us. This subtle restlessness creates stress and unhappiness, an inner awareness that you're not living your life purpose or being true to yourself and a sense that there's more to the story.

Human Design is a powerful tool to
help you remember your story.

Your roadmap to remember why you are here

When you get lost in your Human suit, allow your BodyGraph to be your beacon back home.

Based on a synthesis of Eastern and Western Astrology, the Chinese I'Ching, the Hindu Chakra System, Kabbalah, and Quantum Physics, this powerful system shows you your strengths, your purpose, your gifts and gives you a map to help you realign your life with the true story of Who You Truly Are.

This basic introduction is designed to jog your memory, to push against that inner restlessness that you may feel and to help you answer the most important questions in the world: Who are you? And why are you here?

In this book you'll learn the pieces separately, but the true magic or brilliance is when we put them all back together into a fully synthesized story. May these words begin the start of your journey back to remembering the truth of what you came here to experience, what you came here to do and who you came here to be!

Human Design shows us the Nexus between the Human and Spiritual Experience

Your Human Design Chart is made of two distinctly different aspects: your Soul Purpose and your Life Story (Purpose). The purpose of life is growth and expansion. Our Souls manifest on Earth to experience whatever they need to experience to add to the growth of the Universe.

The Human Design Chart

Your Life Purpose is the story of Who You Are in this incarnation. This story is encoded in your energy blueprint as well as in your genetic and epigenetic lineage. At the moment of your birth, your Soul Purpose integrated with your Life Purpose to create a once-in-a-lifetime event that is YOU!

Over our lives, we often experience struggle between elements of our Soul Purpose and our Life Purpose. These inner struggles are often "pre-scripted" into the story of your life. Many people find that when they really understand their Human Design, they gain a deeper understanding of their own struggles. This awareness helps you gain new levels of self-mastery so that you can fulfill your potential in a richer, more meaningful way.

The Human Design chart, called the BodyGraph is a visual representation of the sum of human possibilities and energies.

The entire archetype of humanity is contained within the structural framework of the Chart. All the possibilities for the expression of being Human appear here.

The BodyGraph shows us the different ways we love, lead, learn, know, grow, sense and so much more. Your Chart shows you your best strategy for making money, having great relationships, being healthy and staying creatively fulfilled.

Your unique Chart helps you understand how you work and how to best make your life work for you. Each individual Chart is a "map" of how you process energy.

6

Your Chart reveals your strengths, your potential weaknesses, your gifts and your talents. Most importantly, your Chart tells the story of who you are, why you are here and how you can live a life that is in alignment with the truth of who you really are.

Each individual chart is calculated using your birth date, time, and place.

The geometric shapes represent the nine centers.

The lines represent the channels.

The numbers represent the gates.

The colors reveal your strengths, your potential weaknesses, your gifts and talents.

If you look closely at the chart you might see some visual evidence of the influencing wisdom behind Human Design. For example, the geometric shapes called centers look very similar to the seven chakras.

If you turn the chart upside down it looks very similar to the Tree of Life from the Kabbalah.

TRANSPERSONAL lines are
energies that are all about experiences in
relationships with others.

INTRAPERSONAL lines are energies that
are self-focused and all about personal
experience and understanding.

Karen Curry Parker
@understandinghumandesign

Or you may notice that 64 numbers appear on the chart. These numbers, called gates, correlate to the 64 hexagrams from the Chinese I'Ching. In the I'Ching, a hexagram is a figure composed of six stacked horizontal lines, where each line is either yang (an unbroken, or solid line), or yin (broken, an open line with a gap in the center).

Though you can see pieces of these ancient wisdom teachings in the chart, Human Design is something new and unique, a new tool to help people in a brand-new way.

It is important to realize that when you look at parts of the chart, they are simply pieces. To make learning about Human Design easier, we have to start first by taking the chart apart, piece by piece, and covering each one by one.

Quantum Human Design

"You are an infinite, powerful Creator, living in a Human story."

Karen Curry Parker

But once you have a handle on how the chart is constructed, and how to read it, the "story," or personal energy map, is revealed when you put all of the pieces together.

The story of each Chart is based on the synthesis of everything in the Chart. Each one is different and unique. It's in the sum total of all the parts of the Chart that your personal energy "map" is revealed.

Human Design involves a lot of data and that's why we break it down into bite size digestible pieces, but understand that by doing so we are taking pieces out of context. It's when we can put all the pieces back together and look at the whole picture, the entire Design in its wholeness, that's when we see the story of the beauty, magnificence and one-of-a-kind magic that you are!

We've been given a great gift, an invaluable insight into what it means to embody this form as a Soul and live out a specific life story.

This blueprint shows us every archetypal theme of what it means to be a Human Being. It shows us our potential, provides answers to our longing questions and gives us full permission to step into our Truth, to live a life unmasked in the realness, unapologetically authentic expressions of our Divine essence and innate nature.

It's so easy to stay hidden, live small and believe we are what we are not, but living in that misalignment literally sucks the life and energy from you and manifests itself as pain. You can only deny your Truth for so long.

The world needs you, all of you, healed and whole, living in alignment with the fullness of your power, fulfilling your purpose of Being Who You Are, that is your gift, your purpose and your contribution to the Collective.

· We ALL have ALL of the Chart ·

Everything in a Human Design Chart represents an archetypal energy that you can express in an infinite number of ways.

The expression of each element of your Chart is operating on a spectrum, it has a high end, a low end and the space in between.

Quantum Human Design

Everything in our Human Design BodyGraph represents an archetypal energy that we can express in an infinite number of ways.

Karen Curry Parker

It's important to remember, we ALL have ALL of the BodyGraph.

#QuantumHumanDesign

@understandinghumandesign

It's important to remember we all have ALL of the Chart. We can experience all of the energies in the Human Design Chart in the high or low expression of the circuitry that's defined in our specific Chart. We experience our definition more consistently than our openness.

We're here to support you in consciously expressing the highest possible potential of your unique energy, the defined themes of your Channels and Gates.

12

Please note, by no means does this book represent the whole picture about you and your unique Design no more than one chromosome would represent your whole biology. You're a magnificent multidimensional being with great depth and complexity. This is just an introduction to understanding the Quantum Human Design Basics or scratching the surface at best.

WHY THE NEW LANGUAGE?

Words create, they endure. They allow for Unity. They transmit. They are the interface between the Divine and the Human. Words are Power. They translate the infinite to the finite. Words are a code for a story. Words carry frequencies of energy and our DNA responds to that language.

When Ra, the founder of Human Design, first shared his transmission of the system, he did so in a way that penetrated and shocked people into waking up. He needed to speak into the 'Not-Self' or the inauthentic Self in order to quickly get people's attention and it worked.

Having personally known and worked with Ra and after over two decades of teaching Human Design, I have been Divinely inspired and guided to do what Ra wasn't given the time to do, because he suddenly passed away from a heart attack in 2011, and that is to respectfully share the flip side of this beautiful tool, to speak and share this knowledge with empowering, higher vibrational frequency language, that I'm calling Quantum Human Design.

Quantum Human Design is a new and transformed Human Design language that is more expansive, empowering, expressive and comes with a more comprehensive understanding. I have deliberately engineered and upgraded the HD vocabulary to a powerful, positive, higher vibrational frequency of energy to help you fully activate your potential.

Quantum Human Design will provide you with a new way to see your Human Design Chart and tell a bigger and better story about what's possible for You!

TYPE, STRATEGY AND EMOTIONAL THEME

Here are the 5 energy **Types** in Quantum Human Design (with the traditional Human Design name in parentheses) and their decision-making **Strategy**.

1. **Initiator (Manifestor)** - inform then initiate
2. **Orchestrator (Projector)** - wait for recognition and invitation
3. **Alchemist (Generator)** - wait to respond
4. **Time Bender (Manifesting Generator)** - wait to respond, envision, inform, then take action
5. **Calibrator (Reflector)** - wait a Lunar cycle

Your Human Design Type shows you exactly how to create and live in a way that is most empowering, fulfilling, dynamic and successful.

Quantum Human Design
Five Energy Types

Initiator
(Manifestor)

Alchemist
(Generator)

Time Bender
(Manifesting Generator)

Orchestrator
(Projector)

Calibrator
(Reflector)

Karen Curry Parker
@understandinghumandesign

Your Type is the hard wiring of your energetic configuration and your unique way of interacting with the world. Each Type has a unique decision making Strategy. Knowing your Type & Strategy can help you develop the confidence and trust in your capacity and ability to make reliable and correct decisions for yourself.

Each Type has a different role and different way of interacting with others and the world.

Most of us aren't raised to really live out the full power and potential of Who we are. We're all powerful Creators, but in order to use our power in the most efficient and best way we need to know and understand how we operate.

Every energy Type in Design has a specific Strategy. A Strategy is a unique way of making decisions and taking action in the world.

Strategy is the MOST IMPORTANT knowledge piece to put into play, practice and experiment with living out in your everyday life.

Quantum Human Design
Strategy by Type

Initiator - inform then initiate
(Manifestor)

Alchemist - wait to respond
(Generator)

Time Bender - wait to respond, envision,
(Manifesting Generator)   inform, take action

Orchestrator - wait for recognition
(Projector)   & invitation

Calibrator - wait a Lunar cycle
(Reflector)

Karen Curry Parker
@understandinghumandesign

18

If you're not following your Strategy it's like trying to build a house and telling the builders to skip pouring the concrete for laying the foundation because you want your house built without it.

Your Strategy is your personal way to make effective decisions in your life, just like laying the correct foundation will allow a sturdy, secure home to be built upon it. These are important key pieces that you choose to commit to or not.

Your Strategy gives you key information about how you operate your Human vehicle in the world, how to make the right choices with less resistance and how to recognize when you are on the right path or out of alignment with your Truth. If you want to live out the fullest expression of your unique Design, following your Strategy according to your Type is the way.

Think about it—if we're all different, a one-size-fits-all approach to creating a happy, successful life doesn't make sense. All people are equally valuable and important, but each of us has our own energetic blueprint and individual style of operating successfully in life. What might work for one person won't necessarily work for another.

The struggle to fit in and embrace society's definition of what is "right" and "successful" is really just about energy. The way we feel about ourselves, the rules and values of society, and the way we react to life are all dictated by our own energy field and the bigger collective energy field.

Following your Strategy will help you to more naturally align with your Life Purpose, minimize the resistance you experience, make strong and healthy decisions that will feel good, more meaningful and joyful to you and you will truly fulfill your Personal Destiny.

· Emotional Theme ·

Each energy Type has an emotional theme, which is simply part of a person's life and brings them lessons as well as opportunities for growth. When you experience your emotional theme in a strong way, it's usually a sign that you are not living true to yourself (in energetic alignment) or you're not following your Strategy. It's always good to take a step back and evaluate your life if you're feeling your emotional theme in a powerful way.

When you live your life according to your Strategy, you lessen the intensity of your experience with your emotional theme. Following your Strategy makes your entire life experience easier and more enjoyable.

The emotional theme is thematic, meaning that you will either be experiencing the emotions of your theme yourself or you may be experiencing them in other people around you who are responding to your behavior.

Quantum Human Design
Emotional Theme

Initiator (Manifestor)
- anger / peace

Alchemist (Generator)
- frustration / satisfaction

Time Bender (Manifesting Generator)
- frustration & anger / peace & satisfaction

Orchestrator (Projector)
- bitterness (depletion) / success

Calibrator (Reflector)
- disappointment / surprise

Karen Curry Parker
@understandinghumandesign

21

· The Initiator ·

Initiator (Manifestor) - 9% of the population

Initiators are the cosmically initiating force on the planet through their connection to the Divine. They are here to get the ball rolling and move onto the next thing.

Initiators have tremendous initiating power, they can start off projects and act independently. Society as a whole has been taught and conditioned to just go out and "do it" or "make it happen", but this type of independent action is exclusive to the Initiator.

Initiators have an Undefined/Open Sacral and therefore, they don't have sustainable energy and are not here to work in a traditional way or the same way as the Alchemists (Generators) and Time Benders (Manifesting Generators). Properly channeled Initiator energy give the other four Types something to respond to.

Many Initiator's struggle to learn how to use their power appropriately and may have been conditioned to hide their power or suppress their initiation energy since they were small children.

Initiators have an internal, non-verbal creative flow and in order to eliminate the resistance from those around them, they need to inform the people who will be affected by their actions before they act. This simple act of informing builds trust and paves the way for them to move freely and without resistance.

Spiritual Purpose: Translate Divine inspiration into action.

Quantum Purpose: To initiate people into the frequency of transformation and creativity through direct access to the Quantum Pulse.

Strategy: Inform others before taking action

Emotional Theme: Anger-due to creative flow disruption. They naturally have an internal non-verbal creative flow.

Potential Challenges: Reclaiming and living in their power and being patient when things seem to not be moving fast enough.

· The Alchemist ·

Alchemist (Generator) - 37% of the population

Alchemists are the workforce and life-force energy on the planet, the builders and doers of the world.

They're here to become masters of what they respond to do and create. If they're patient and wait to respond to what shows up in their outer reality, instead of trying to figure things out with their mind in regard to what they should be doing, they'll become fully activated in their purpose.

Alchemists may feel frustrated often because they know they're here to do something that fulfills their full potential and things aren't moving fast enough. They're conditioned by the world to use their thinking and the power of their mind to set their path to mastery, BUT the truth is that their path is revealed to them by the world outside of them!

It takes faith and understanding on how to connect to that path correctly to align themselves with their destiny and ultimate fulfillment of their potential. Alchemists need to wait for things to show up in their outer reality that is a sign and confirmation that it's the right idea to take action on.

Spiritual Purpose: Turn inspiration into form.

Quantum Purpose: To physically manifest creativity and express through devotion.

Strategy: Wait to respond. Wait for something to show up in their outer reality in order for them to respond to.

Emotional Theme: Frustration due to momentum. They may not feel like things are moving fast enough for them. They have a stair-step learning curve and will hit plateaus, but encourage them to not give up or quit completely, they'll eventually have a breakthrough and reach mastery.

Potential Challenge: Endurance and waiting on Divine Timing.

· The Time Bender ·

Time Bender (Manifesting Generator) - 33% of the population

Time Benders are a hybrid of the Initiator (Manifestor) and Alchemist (Generator). They are the workforce, life-force energy, builders and doers of the world like the Alchemists, however, they also have some traits of the Initiator like the internal non-verbal creative flow and taking action, <u>BUT</u> only after they've followed their Strategy of waiting to respond.

It's correct for the Time Bender to be doing many things at once (multi-tasking) while they are waiting for something to show up in their outer reality for them to respond to.

They move fast and skip steps to find the fastest and most efficient way to the end result *(sometimes they may have to go back and complete the steps they skipped if they find them to be important.)*

They have a deep inner awareness to know what's right for them, a strong intuition turned on by gut level responses that will place them in the right place at the right time, doing the right work and having the right impact.

Spiritual Purpose: Turn inspiration into form.

Quantum Purpose: To physically manifest creativity and speed up the Quantum process and linear time. They find the places where they can skip steps, therefore creating shortcuts and expediting the process. Shortcuts = bending time. They shift the way we do things and are able to manifest more than one thing at a time.

Strategy: Wait to respond, envision, inform, then take action.

Emotional Theme: Frustration and Anger due to creative flow disruption and momentum. They have an internal non-verbal creative flow like the Initiator (Manifestor). They have a place where they are so intimately connected to Source and the Quantum Field that they are directly moving through the Quantum Field. This is possible only in response.

Potential Challenge: Sense of aloneness and disconnection from Spirit and learning how to surrender to Time! They can influence time, but they cannot control it. They need to get into alignment with time to minimize the momentum of the energy of frustration. Learn to let go of attachment to time and surrender to Universal timing.

· The Orchestrator ·

Orchestrator (Projector) - 20% of the population

Orchestrators are the ones who get and sense the necessary information and resources others need. Having an Open/Undefined Sacral Center, they are not here to work in the traditional 9-5 way, especially if it's physical labor.

They're here to lead, guide, direct and manage "their people", the ones who see, recognize, value and invite them; otherwise they will be losing and leaking energy.

Orchestrators have the energy for 'their people', to guide and direct them, not to do the work themselves. Some believe they can initiate and do more than they're capable of because they're taking in the Sacral energy (work-force/life-force energy) of others and amplifying it. But it's not sustainable for them to hold onto this energy, those who do will experience burnout, (a lot of Orchestrators experience burnout at age 40.)

Orchestrators are also constantly taking in the energy of the entire Planet Earth in their energy field. Even if they're sitting on the couch watching Netflix, they're clearing and transmuting all of the hurting on the Planet and creating a new template. They're moving things on the ethereal plane.

Spiritual Purpose: To anchor the energetic template of what we are here to create, to align the energy of the world and heal the energy of the planet.

Quantum Purpose: To hold the energy template of what's to come and to clear the vibration of the Collective Consciousness.

Strategy: Wait for recognition and invitation for the big things in life:

Friendships & Romance

Career / Work Opportunities

Where to Live

Always wait to be invited or asked before sharing their gift of guidance & direction with others.

Emotional Theme: Depletion. They're here to experience mastery through guiding not through working. They may even feel bitter if they're not being recognized and rewarded for their wisdom and contribution, but that's just showing them who are NOT their people. Their people will see them and their value. They will gladly take their guidance, direction and wisdom. Their people will find them, they will be invited, they need to remember to be patient and trust in the process of Divine Timing.

Potential Challenge: Self-worth and energy, feeling abandoned by Spirit.

· The Calibrator ·

Calibrator (Reflector) - 1% of the population

Calibrators are wise, intuitive, empathic and sensitive Lunar Beings. They are fully open to the world and to others. They sense and feel the potential of Humanity.

Because they have no defined Centers by Design, they take in the energy of everybody else and see the world through others eyes, sampling a frequency of energy and reflecting it back. They magnify and reflect all that is around them and mirror it back for others. It's through the reflection of what they are showing the world that shows up and shows us what we need to recalibrate.

It's essential for Calibrators to choose their partners and friends carefully because they will have a huge impact on their feelings and experience of themselves. Like the other Open/Undefined Sacral Types, Initiators (Manifestors) and Orchestrators (Projectors), they are not here to work in the traditional way like the Alchemists (Generators) and Time Benders (Manifesting Generators), who have Defined Sacral's.

They may feel alone and misunderstood and also feel deep disappointment with having to wait and live through the energy of others. It is not correct for Calibrators to make decisions with their mind or like the other Types. They need to experience a choice or decision over a cycle of the Moon (29 days).

They experience this choice or decision inside of themselves through talking it out over the entire Moon cycle and this gives them the power to be able to realize solutions and the right choices.

Spiritual Purpose: To be the barometer of the alignment of humanity with Heart.

Quantum Purpose: To mirror to others the Human condition and Human potential. It's vital for them to geographically be in the right place with the right people.

Strategy: Waiting 29 days, one full Lunar cycle to make their decisions. They need and will get clarity over time.

Emotional Theme: Disappointment due to witnessing the unfulfilled potential and the need for more time.

Potential Challenge: The courage to extricate from the misaligned and faith. Meaning they see the potential in others so strongly that sometimes they will stay in places and relationships longer than is good, healthy or in their best interest.

AUTHORITY

Although decision making is tied directly to your Strategy, your Authority flavors the way you use your Strategy. Your Defined Centers will determine your Authority. Not all centers carry Authority, so your personal Authority will depend on your Type and your Definition.

Authority will also depend on your life conditioning and your level of emotional well-being. When you receive a Human Design reading, you are taught to understand patterns of pain and behaviors that may be keeping you from living out the beauty of the mythology of who you really are.

With cognitive awareness of old patterns, you begin to heal and transform these energies into deep sources of wisdom, the more you clear your old energy patterns, the more effectively your natural decision making skills (your Authority) can function. You can then begin to use your Authority along with your Strategy to help you make better decisions for your life.

It's very important to note that Authority does not override your Strategy, it just shifts the way you use your Strategy so that your decisions and choices are even more in alignment with the overall energy in your Design.

Seven kinds of Authority:

- Sacral

- Splenic

- Emotional Solar Plexus

- Ego (Will)

- Self-Projected

- Mental-Projected

- Lunar

Initiators (Manifestors), Orchestrators (Projectors), Alchemists (Generators) and Time Benders (Manifesting Generators) all have Authority in their Design. Calibrators (Reflectors), because they have no Centers defined in their Design, have no true Authority other than their Calibrator Strategy, which is to wait a full Lunar cycle.

Sacral Authority - Sacral Authority means that you have a defined Sacral Center and that there are no additional energies influencing your Sacral. Your Sacral is the only decision-making center in your Design, and your Sacral response in the moment is the correct Authority for you at any given point in time.

Sacral Authority

Sacral Authority means that you have a defined Sacral Center and that there are no additional energies influencing your Sacral.

- Karen Curry Parker

Alchemists commonly use a whole range of sacral sounds whic1h express likes and dislikes, consent or discontent. "Uh-huh" and "uh-uh/un-un", or "mmh" when undecided, are all sacral sounds that are great tools for recognizing energetic response before, during or after an activity.

Most will come naturally to Alchemists unless they have been conditioned to suppress or ignore them. Listening for sounds or tuning into your gut feeling is imperative as this will clearly indicate how to expend your energy in a satisfactory way.

Side note: Because the response of a 34/20 Time Bender (Manifesting Generator) is so fast it tends to bypass the sacral sounds and they will just respond with a "yes" or "no" or a "yeah", "yup" or "nope" and that is correct for them.

35

Splenic Authority - The Spleen is the center for survival, time, health, and intuition. Because it is the energy for basic survival, it is very time-centered and always operates with an intuitive pulse in the moment. You trust your gut and act on it. This is pretty easy for Initiators (Manifestors) and Orchestrators (Projectors), but sometimes it can be confusing for Alchemists (Generators), who may wonder if their spleen overrides their Sacral response.

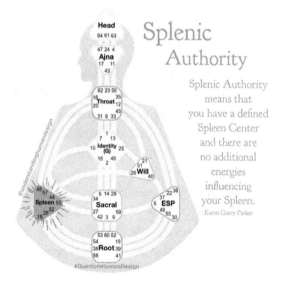

Splenic
Authority

Splenic Authority
means that
you have a defined
Spleen Center
and there are
no additional
energies
influencing
your Spleen.
- Karen Curry Parker

For Alchemists with Splenic Authority, their Sacral response in the moment is correct. Your Spleen and your Sacral actually work together.

36

Emotional Solar Plexus Authority - Approximately half of the population has emotional Authority— which means they need to ride the wave of their shifting emotions to come to a place of clarity.

When you have a Defined Emotional Solar Plexus, it will dramatically influence your Strategy. The Defined Emotional Solar Plexus is a Motor with energy that pulses in waves. If you are emotionally Defined, you probably know that you have moods or changes in your emotional energy pretty regularly.

Emotional
Solar Plexus
Authority

Emotional Solar Plexus
Authority means
that you have a
defined Emotional
Solar Plexus (ESP)
Center and there
are no additional
energies influencing
your Emotional
Solar Plexus.
- Karen Curry Parker

It's pretty common for emotionally defined people to be terrified of making decisions. They often have a history of enthusiastically leaping into decisions and then waking up a few days later only to find that their mood has shifted and now they are obligated to finish a project or a relationship that they just aren't in the mood for anymore.

If you have a defined Emotional Solar Plexus, you are not here to be spontaneous, though others will often put pressure on you to leap into things. Leaping into things without waiting for clarity will only create chaos in your life if you have emotional Authority.

When you have emotional Authority in your Design, you still use your Strategy, but you need to wait until it feels right. Avoid premature action when under pressure. Patience allows you to experience the "wave," or swing of moods and emotions. Giving yourself the appropriate amount of time to process your emotions allows you to make your decisions from a place of calm and clarity.

Ego (Will) Authority - Only Initiators (Manifestors) have Ego Manifested Authority. Ego Manifested Authority is when your Will Center is connected via a colored channel to your Throat Center.

Orchestrators (Projectors) can have Ego Projected Authority. This is when the Will Center is connected via a colored channel to your Identity (G) Center. This is very rare! Follow your Orchestrator Strategy!

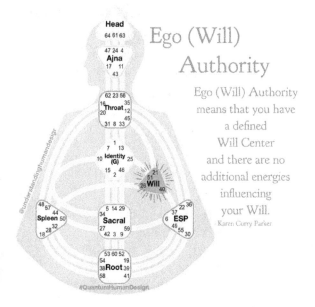

Ego (Will) Authority

Ego (Will) Authority means that you have a defined Will Center and there are no additional energies influencing your Will.

Karen Curry Parker

The Will Center is a motor that works to rest and the cycle repeats, so it's important that you are honoring your energy, that you're well rested and you're not making decisions from a place of burnout. It can be easy, with having willpower, to push through burnout and actually damage your health even further. If you have Ego Manifested or Ego Projected Authority, check in with yourself to see if you need some downtime before you say 'yes' or make another commitment.

Self-Projected Authority - Only Orchestrators (Projectors) have self-projected authority. Self-projected authority comes from a channel connecting the Identity Center to the Throat Center with no other overriding energies defined in your Design, such as the Emotional Solar Plexus or the Spleen.

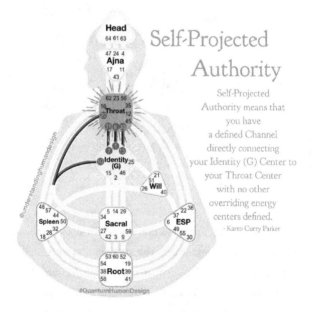

Self-Projected
Authority

Self-Projected
Authority means that
you have
a defined Channel
directly connecting
your Identity (G) Center to
your Throat Center
with no other
overriding energy
centers defined.
- Karen Curry Parker

Self-Projected Authority means that you have to talk to other people to get clarity about which invitations are right for you. You have to "see" your decisions reflected or projected through others in order to really know what is correct for you.

It would benefit you greatly to have one or two close people that you can just talk things out with so you can get clarity through your talking and that aren't going to 'tell you what to do' or try to give you their advice. You just need to hear yourself talk to get clarity on making decisions in your life, you and the other person you're talking to having this awareness will be greatly beneficial and way less frustrating because they'll know they're just giving you a safe space to talk things out, without actually trying to give you their input, advice or tell you what to do.

Mental Projected Authority - Mental Projected Authority is only experienced by Orchestrators (Projectors) as well. Mental Projected Authority comes from a Channel connecting the Ajna to the Throat Center with no other overriding energies defined in the Chart, such as the Emotional Solar Plexus or the Spleen.

Mental-Projected Authority

Mental-Projected Authority means that you have a defined Channel directly connecting your Ajna Center to your Head Center (or Ajna to Throat Center) with no other overriding energy centers defined.

- Karen Curry Parker

Just like Self-Projected Authority, Mental Projected Authority means that you have to talk to other people to get clarity about which invitations are right for you. You have to "see" your decisions reflected or projected through others in order to really know what is correct for you.

And just like Self-Projected Authority, it would benefit you greatly to have one or two close people that you can just talk things out with so you can get clarity through your talking and that aren't going to 'tell you what to do' or try to give you their advice.

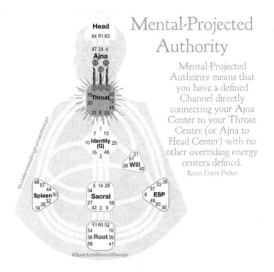

Mental-Projected Authority

Mental-Projected Authority means that you have a defined Channel directly connecting your Ajna Center to your Throat Center (or Ajna to Head Center) with no other overriding energy centers defined.

– Karen Curry Parker

You just need to hear yourself talk to get clarity on making decisions in your life, you and the other person you're talking to having this awareness will be greatly beneficial and way less frustrating because they'll know they're just giving you a safe space to talk things out, without actually trying to give you their input, advice or tell you what to do.

Lunar Authority - Calibrators (Reflectors) Only - When there are no Centers Defined in a Chart, we have a Calibrator whose personal Authority is established by the way their Design connects to the lunar cycle. A reliable and repeatable

43

pattern is created as the Moon transits each of the 64 Gates around the Mandala every 29 days for as long they live.

Before making an important decision, Calibrators need to spend at least one lunar cycle contemplating and discussing the issue or situation. If they understand their Strategy and rely on their Lunar Authority, they can achieve clarity in their decision-making process and feel confident about their decision.

Just like the Orchestrators (Projectors) with Self-Projected or Mental Projected Authority need to do, Calibrators would also greatly benefit from having one or two close people that they can just talk things out with so they can get clarity through talking and know that these people are not going to 'tell them what to do' or try to give them their advice.

As a Calibrator you just need to take your time and hear yourself talk things out to get clarity through the length of the Lunar cycle. A key for Calibrators is to slow down and not let the world rush them.

THE NINE CENTERS

The first thing you may notice when you look at your Chart is that there are nine geometric shapes. These are called the Nine Centers.

Each Center carries and manages a certain frequency of energy and relates to specific themes in our lives.

· The Transition from 7-Centered to 9-Centered Beings ·

With the discovery of the planet Uranus by Herschel in 1781, we moved into the Uranian Era when Human Beings with highly evolved 9-centered forms began replacing 7-centered, mind-oriented Beings. By the late 1800's the process was complete, making all of us alive today 9-centered Beings.

This means in the traditional Chakra system the Heart Chakra split into the Identity (G) Center & Will Center. And the Solar Plexus Chakra split into the Emotional Solar Plexus Center & Spleen Center.

Transition from 7-Centered to 9-Centered Beings

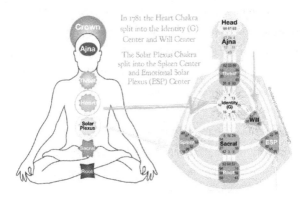

In 1781 the Heart Chakra split into the Identity (G) Center and Will Center

The Solar Plexus Chakra split into the Spleen Center and Emotional Solar Plexus (ESP) Center

This historically significant moment in our evolution marked the movement away from our need to focus on survival through the mental awareness or mental intelligence of the strategic mind.

The 7-centered Beings had a shorter life expectancy marked by the Saturnian cycle. Our new 9-centered forms or bodies have an 84-year life expectancy marked by the Uranian cycle.

7-centered Beings were driven to find connection and communion through sexuality because of the need and desire to reproduce whereas, now being 9-centered Beings, we are finding connection and communion through awareness.

Our now highly evolved 9-centered body vehicle is designed to guide us through life decision by decision, meaning we no longer need to look to an outer authority through our mind for direction. There are no answers in our mind, only infinite possibilities.

Understanding our Human Design Type, Strategy, and Authority, allows us to make decisions that are correctly in alignment with our most Authentic Self, which then, as we practice this, allows us to trust ourselves more and more.

· Defined Centers ·

If a Center is colored, then it is called Defined. A Defined Center has a consistent way of operating and is part of the energy you consistently express. This is the energy that you radiate out into the world.

It operates the same way energetically and thematically. This is the aspects of your personality that are true all the time, independent of any other factors in your environment.

Your definition is determined by what Gates the Planets were transiting in at the moment of your birth. Your definition will stay the same throughout your lifetime.

49

The beauty of our Defined and Undefined Centers is that individually we are all puzzle pieces--parts of a greater whole. We all become completely Defined when we are all together.

We each bring pieces that energetically unify us all and offer us the opportunity to express all of the Human experience.

We all have ALL of the Chart, it's just that what is Defined in your Chart is what you consistently experience, radiate and express all the time no matter where you are, who you're with are where the planets are transiting.

The way that you are Defined and your specific configuration (energetic hard-wiring) is completely unique to you and you alone, there is no one else exactly like you on the planet, similar...sure, but not exactly like you.

You're a once in a lifetime event and that makes you rare, precious, special and an INVALUABLE VITAL GIFT to the entire planet! I'm wondering if you think of and see yourself this way?

· Open/Undefined Centers ·

If a Center is white, then it is called Undefined or Open.

Undefined Center = A white Center with at least one Gate activation (Hanging Gate).

Open Center = A white Center with no Gate activation (Hanging Gates).

Undefined/Open Centers are where we take in energy and Information from the world around us. We not only absorb energies in our openness, but we also AMPLIFY them.

In our openness, we experience other people's energies and because of this, we have the potential for great wisdom, but also the potential for pain and confusion. It's in our openness that we have been deeply conditioned, by family, friends and society.

These Undefined or Open areas represent aspects of your personality that are inconsistent because it changes depending on who you're around. This can also feel more intense than defined energy, because it's always changing and you're amplifying it.

It's easy to think the energy in your Open or Undefined Centers is yours, and sometimes you will try to "fix" an aspect of your personality or wonder "what's wrong with me?", not realizing that you're behaving according to outside factors that isn't even really you!

Your openness is where you have the potential for the most pain until you understand how your energy works; until you learn what's you/yours and what's not you/yours.

When you learn what energy is yours and what isn't yours is when your openness starts to become the place for your greatest wisdom. You learn that you're only experiencing this energy and it's not what defines you. You're then able to experience the energy and let it go.

Are you aware of the areas you've been conditioned? Having this awareness starts the seven year deconditioning process.

· The Quantum Interface (Head) Center ·

The Defined Head Center is colored in yellow. Because the energy in the Defined Head Center is always "on", people with Defined Head Centers are inspirational forces on the planet. They're always radiating inspiration out into the world and may not even be aware of it because it's happening energetically, but it's happening.

Defined Head Centers have a consistent source of inspiration. The are always asking questions and may feel like something's wrong, feel confusion or struggle to know what to do if they don't have the answers.

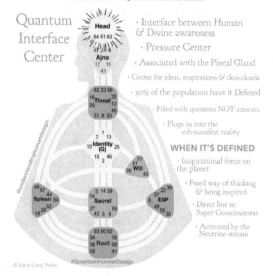

Quantum
Interface
Center

· Interface between Human
  & Divine awareness
· Pressure Center
· Associated with the Pineal Gland
· Center for ideas, inspirations & downloads
· 30% of the population have it Defined
· Filled with questions NOT answers
· Plugs us into the
  sub-manifest reality

WHEN IT'S DEFINED
· Inspirational force on
  the planet
· Fixed way of thinking
  & being inspired
· Direct line to
  Super Consciousness
· Activated by the
  Neutrino stream

© Karen Curry Parker   #QuantumHumanDesign

Inspiration is a reflective process, it's important to process the questions you are receiving, but DON'T rely on the answers to make decisions about your life, follow your Strategy!

Oftentimes people with Defined Head Centers don't realize that they're even questioning things. They may even have a permanent quizzical look on their face, it's simply a part of their consistent energy.

54

Affirmation for your Defined Head: "I am inspired and inspiring. I spread inspiration everywhere I go and I share my ideas and inspirations with others according to my Strategy."

Someone with an Open/Undefined Head Center does not have a consistent way to receive inspiration, so when they come across inspiration they will take it in and amplify it. It's very easy when you have an Open/Undefined Head Center to feel inspired all the time. Not only do you feel inspired, but you also feel pressure to act on this inspiration.

Quantum Interface Center

Head
64 61 63
47
Ajna
17 11
43

· Interface between Human & Divine awareness

· Pressure Center

· Associated with the Pineal Gland

· Center for ideas, inspirations & downloads

· 70% of the population have it Open/Undefined

· Filled with questions NOT answers

· Plugs us into the sub-manifest reality

WHEN IT'S OPEN/UNDEFINED

· Energy comes from environment, people & planets

· Pressure to figure things out

· Wise about ideas & inspirations

· Use your Strategy to know which ideas to take action on

62 23 56
16   35
Throat 12
20
45
31 8 33

1   13
7
10 Identity 25
     (G)
15   46
    2

21
51
26 Will
    40

48 57
44
Spleen 50
18 28 32

5 14 29
34
Sacral
27   59
42 3 9

37   22 36
6 ESP
49 55
      30

53 60 52
54   19
38 Root 39
58   41

©understandinghumandesign

#QuantumHumanDesign

© Karen Curry Parker

Those who understand their Open/Undefined Head Center can have a very deep understanding of who and what is truly inspiring. They can be wise about which inspirations to take action on and which to simply observe.

Not only will someone with an Open/Undefined Head Center have the ability to take in the inspiration of the world and amplify it, but they'll also take in all the questions of the world and amplify those too.

Remember, you do not need to answer any of the questions. The only thing you really need to do to make good decisions is to follow your Strategy!

The purpose is not to try and figure things out, it's to use the power of your daydreams and imagination, your creative thinking, to stimulate emotional energy. That emotional energy in turn calibrates your Heart Center and the electromagnetic resonance field of the heart creates a vibrational frequency that attracts into your life things that match that particular frequency of creativity.

Calibrating emotional energy and using the power of your thoughts maintains and sustains a high quality emotional frequency of energy to support you in creating what you want in your life.

✦ **Question to ask yourself (Open/Undefined Head):** "Am I under pressure to answer other people's questions and live out their ideas and inspirations?"

✦ **Affirmation for your Open/Undefined Head:** "I am deeply inspired all the time. I am wise about what is truly inspiring. I follow my Strategy to help me decide what I need to do. The questions in my head are from others. I don't have to answer all of them. Only the ones that truly excite me!"

· The Divine Translator (Ajna) Center ·

The Defined Ajna Center is colored in green. The Defined Ajna is designed to hold information. It is trustworthy and reliable, but it is fixed in how it works. It's important to remember that the mind is a great resource, but it is NOT a place to make decisions, no decisions should come from the mind. That's what your Strategy & inner-authority is for (Strategy for Calibrators since they don't have an inner-authority).

If your Ajna is Defined, try playing and experimenting in your relationships to only share or speak what's on your mind if you're asked to share or if someone asks you what you think, especially if it's giving your opinion. This works both ways, you can also ask, *"Hey, would you like to hear what I think?"* Or *"Can I share something that's on my mind with you?"* You may find that what you have to say is more well received.

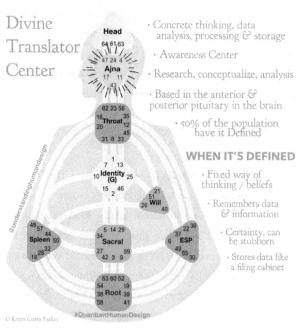

Divine Translator Center

- Concrete thinking, data analysis, processing & storage
- Awareness Center
- Research, conceptualize, analysis
- Based in the anterior & posterior pituitary in the brain
- 50% of the population have it Defined

WHEN IT'S DEFINED

- Fixed way of thinking / beliefs
- Remembers data & information
- Certainty, can be stubborn
- Stores data like a filing cabinet

© Karen Curry Parker #QuantumHumanDesign

@understandinghumandesign

58

Affirmation for your Defined Ajna: "I am gentle with my thinking and always remember that there are many ways to think about information. I am uniquely capable of being certain. I listen carefully to the thoughts of others and allow for limitless thinking with grace."

Someone with an Open/Undefined Ajna Center can see many sides to an issue. They are fair, judicious, empathetic, open-minded and can be very intellectual.

An Open/Undefined Ajna doesn't have a fixed way of thinking, so they are able to process and understand information in a myriad of ways. People with an Open/ Undefined Ajna, who are able to relax, can become great mind readers.

Because the Open/Undefined Ajna is designed to take in information and ideas and see all the different layers and levels of understanding, it can be a challenge to "lock on to" a fixed idea or belief. With great effort people with Open/ Undefined Ajna's can hold a fixed idea, but it doesn't come easily or naturally.

Divine Translator Center

Head

64 61 63
47 24 4
Ajna
17 11
43

62 23 56
16 35
Throat 12
20
45
31 8 33

1
7 13
10 Identity 25
(G)
15 46
2
21
51
26 Will 40

48 57
44
Spleen 50
28 32
18

5 14 29
34
Sacral
27 59
42 3 9

22 36
37
6 ESP
49 55 30

53 60 52
54 19
38 Root 39
58 41

© Karen Curry Parker

@understandinghumandesign

#QuantumHumanDesign

· Concrete thinking, data analysis, processing & storage

· Awareness Center

· Research, conceptualize, analysis

· Based in the anterior & posterior pituitary in the brain

· 50% of the population have it Open/Undefined

WHEN IT'S OPEN/UNDEFINED

· Designed to be open-minded, unlimited perspectives

· Wise about data & analysis

· Struggle with certainty & to remember data

· Wisdom to see things from many perspectives

· Tries to hold onto fixed ideas & beliefs

You may have been told that you need to just make up your mind about something and stick to it. Remember that you are here to be wise about ideas and beliefs, but not necessarily adopt them. The beliefs that you hold on to will be the ones you came to through using your Human Design Strategy and Authority.

Question to ask yourself (Open/Undefined Ajna):
"Am I struggling with making up my mind or feeling confident

in my decisions? Am I trying to convince others and myself that I am certain?"

Affirmation for your Open Ajna: "I am wise about information and beliefs. My gift is that I can see many sides of an issue and have many different understandings that are fluid and that change all the time. I don't have to make up my mind. I always write down the things I want to remember."

· The Activation (Throat) Center ·

The Defined Throat is colored in brown. It is designed to speak, but how it speaks is controlled by what it is connected to. Effective communication is vital for personal and global well-being. Experiment with living your Strategy and see how it improves the quality of your relationships.

Throat Connections

It's vital to to enter into communication correctly.

Initiators (Manifestors) and Time Benders (Manifesting Generators) can initiate speaking.

Alchemists (Generators) need to wait to respond to speak. You work and relate (you speak and act on the responsive sounds of the Sacral about work and relationships).

Orchestrators (Projectors) need to wait to be invited to speak.

Calibrators (Reflectors) also need to be asked (or invited/called out/recognized) to speak as well.

Activation Center

Head
64 61 63

· Center for communication & manifestation

Ajna
47 24 4
17 11
43

· Energy modulation & regulation

· Represents the Thyroid & Parathyroid

62 23 56
16 35
Throat 12
20 45
31 8 33

· 70% of the population have it Defined

WHEN IT'S DEFINED

7 13
10 **Identity (G)** 25
15 46
2

· Ajna to Throat - you speak your mind

· G to Throat - you speak from the depth of Who You Are, your Soul

21
51
26 **Will** 40

· Will to Throat - you speak using the pronoun "I"

· ESP to Throat - you speak what you feel

48 57
44
Spleen 50
18 32
28

5 14 29
34
Sacral
27 69
42 3 9

22 36
37
6 **ESP**
49 55
30

· Root to Throat - you speak about what you do

· Spleen to Throat - you speak what you sense

53 60 52
54 19
38 **Root** 39
58 41

· Sacral to Throat - you speak about work & your relationships

@understandinghumandesign

© Karen Curry Parker
#QuantumHumanDesign

Throat Connection Themes

Ajna to the Throat: you speak your mind (but should only when you are asked & invited!)

Spleen to the Throat: you talk about what you sense (highly intuitive or wants to go deep)

G to the Throat: you are what you talk about, speaking from the depth of who you are, your Soul (can be very vulnerable and sensitive to criticism, as your creative expression comes straight from your Identity. If you're judged for who you are, you can go into a shell like a turtle & shutdown)

Will to the Throat: you talk about yourself, "I this, I that" (me, me, me/potential to be in Ego or surrender who you are to serve others - deep service and providing resources for others, but will always talk using the pronoun I)

Solar Plexus to the Throat: you talk about what you feel (can speak about your emotions easily)

Root to the Throat: you talk about what you do (the drive to do / timing and sense)

Tip: Projected energy (non-motorized energy) needs to be invited or asked to speak in order to be heard.

Affirmation for your Defined Throat: "I speak with great responsibility and know the true source of my words. I allow others to have a voice and I use my words to invite others to share."

People with an Open/Undefined Throat always feel under pressure to speak. When they are in a group or in school this can be very difficult. The Open/Undefined Throat often blurts out comments or answers—sometimes uncontrollably, unaware of where the comment came from (this is even worse if your Ajna is also Open/Undefined).

Activation Center

Head
64 61 63

Ajna
47 24 4
17 11
43

62 23 56
16   35
Throat
20   12
45
31 8 33

7 13
Identity (G)
10   25
15 2 46

21
Will
26   40

Spleen
48 57
50
18 28 32

5 14 29
34
Sacral
27   59
42 3 9

22 36
37
6 **ESP**
49 55
30

53 60 52
54   19
Root
38   39
58   41

© Karen Curry Parker
#QuantumHumanDesign
@understandinghumandesign

· Center for communication & manifestation

· Energy modulation & regulation

· Represents the Thyroid & Parathyroid

· 30% of the population have it Open/Undefined

WHEN IT'S OPEN/UNDEFINED

· Struggle for recognition, attention & speaking the truth

· Often feels invisible & seeks attention

· Needs access to energy

· Can talk too much because they haven't felt heard

· Designed for silence, but under pressure from the energy they're taking in

· Wait to be recognized & asked or invited to speak

· Here to be wise about communication & action

· Often great at impersonations or changing the way their voice sounds

There is, however, deep wisdom in the Open/Undefined Throat. Many great singers (like Celine Dion) and well-known speakers (like Oprah Winfrey) have Open/Undefined Throat Centers. Someone with an Open/Undefined Throat can speak in various ways depending on who they are with. They can be very good at speaking foreign languages and impersonating others' speech.

In order for the Open/Undefined Throat and the thyroid to remain healthy, it is important to speak according to your Strategy. Try experimenting with not talking, don't say a thing unless you're given something to respond to or you are invited into a conversation. If you are silent, your aura does the talking! Just wait and see. People won't be able to stop themselves from talking to you!

✦ **Question to ask yourself (Open/Undefined Throat):** "Am I trying to get attention so that I can be heard?"

✦ **Affirmation for your Open/Undefined Throat:** "My words are heard best when I am invited to speak. I save my words for people who truly desire to hear my point of view and insights. I wait for the right people to ask me and value my words."

· The Calibration (Identity/G) Center ·

In 1781 the Heart Chakra split in two, the Identity (G) Center & Will Center.

We calibrate our heart by virtue of the quality of love that we are experiencing for ourselves and in our lives. Not just love, love and acceptance. Self-Love and Self-Acceptance really are the big energies associated with the G Center.

Self-acceptance is really the theme of the Soul curriculum when our G Center is Defined. Both Self-Love and Self-Acceptance are calibrated by the Gates of the G Center.

We are designed to take our direction in life or what we attract into our life based on the magnetic resonance field of our heart that is an attractive force otherwise known as the Magnetic Monopole.

We attract into our life things that match the quality of Love that we have. The highest expression of all the archetypes amplifies the potential direction that our life takes us.

Calibration Center

Head
64 61 63

47 24 4
Ajna
17 11
43

62 23 56
16 · Throat · 35
20 · 12
45
31 8 33

7 13
10 Identity 25
(G)
15 46
2
21
51 Will
28 40

48 57
44
Spleen 50
32
28
18

5 14 29
34
Sacral
27 59
42 3 9

22 36
37
6 ESP
49 55 30

53 60 52
54 19
38 Root 39
58 41

· Center for Self, identity, love & direction
· Magnetic Monopole resides here
· Attracts things to you that are a part of your life purpose
· Associated with the liver & blood
· 55% of the population have it Defined

WHEN IT'S DEFINED

· Here to give love
· Decisive and Self-accepting
· Has a sense of Self
· Asks if they can be loved & accepted for who they are?

@understandinghumandesign

© Karen Curry Parker   #QuantumHumanDesign

The more we know and understand these energies and live out the optimal expressions the richer our life gets and the richer the things we attract gets.

Love, in one form or another, is what life is all about. This feeling of separation is what drives us to look outside ourselves for love, trying to get a sense of where we are going and who we are in relation to others. We are trying to become worthy of the illusive love we seek.

The truth is that everything has been right here within us all along; we do not have to look outside ourselves to discover who we are, or where to go to find Love. The G Center holds Love. Love is the force that permeates and binds the universe, pulling everything toward a state of oneness again.

Surrendering to the direction of our form is how we are designed to experience the fullness of that Love. We are not here to be loved, but to BE Love.

Affirmation for your Defined Identity (G) Center: "I am who I am. I express myself in all that I do. I celebrate the magnificence of who I am."

The aspects or archetypes that influence the kind of Love we are experiencing (or not) in our lives include the following:

Gate 10: Self-Love - empowering others to love themselves by example.

Gate 7: Collaboration - Natural ability to support a leader in fulfilling their role to better serve the people they're leading. (Chief of Staff energy)

Gate 1: Purpose - Wisdom to realize that the full expression of your unique potential IS the creative gift you give to the world.

Gate 13: Narrative - Capacity to craft a powerful personal narrative and doing forgiveness work. Hearing and holding stories of others, finding the gifts in the stories and taking those blessings from the past to use as a source of growth and expansion to reframe the story that serves the Highest good and well-being of all.

The Calibration Center

Purpose
I Am.
I Am Who I Am.

Collaboration
I am powerful.
I decide. I choose.

Narrative
I am forgiving.
I forgive.

1
7   13

Self-Love
I am Love.
I love.

10   Identity
(G)
Center   25

Spirit
I am trusting.
I trust. I serve.

15   46
2

Compassion
I am compassionate.
I share.

Embodiment
I am vital.
I embody my Spirit/Soul.

Allowing
I am supported.
I receive.

Gate 25: Spirit (Trusting the Universe) - Direction in life that is influenced by trusting the Universe and knowing you are Loved by Spirit and the Universe. Ability to find the Spiritual blessing and connection in every aspect of life. Healing by remembering your connection to Spirit and surrendering the Ego (Self) to your Higher Self (Soul).

Gate 46: Embodiment - Recognition that your body is the vehicle for your Soul. Loving your body and holding your physical form as a sacred vessel for the essence of your Soul and to embody in your vessel the sacredness of Who You Are, to fully experience and express the full vitality of Spirit in form.

Gate 2: Allowing - Ability to allow and receive greater and greater things because you are worth it and deserve it. To value, love and accept yourself and align with being fully supported by the Universe in all the ways you need in order to fulfill your life purpose.

Gate 15: Compassion - A place of compassion and love for Self and others. Following the flow of natural order and finding the place to serve the greatest needs.

We're designed to take our direction in life or what we attract into our life based on the magnetic resonance field of our heart that is an attractive force otherwise known as the Magnetic Monopole.

People with an Open/Undefined Identity Center understand other people's sense of Self and direction. They'll take in another person's identity and amplify it, giving them insight into another person's perspective.

It is extremely important for people with Open/Undefined Identity Centers to geographically be in the right place and with the right people. How they express themselves may change depending on who they are experiencing at the moment.

Because a person with an Open/Undefined Identity Center has a dynamic sense of themselves and their own personal direction, often they can be afraid that they're not lovable. Who they perceive themselves to be is always changing and therefore how they receive love is also always changing. Children with an Open/Undefined Identity Center may also sometimes be a little bit more vulnerable to self-esteem issues.

Calibration Center

Head
64 61 63

47 24 4
Ajna
17 11
43

62 23 56
16 **Throat** 35
20 12
45
31 8 33

1 7 13
10 **Identity (G)** 25
15 46
2
21 51
26 **Will** 40

48 57
44
Spleen 50
16 28 32
18

5 14 29
34
Sacral
27 59
42 3 9

37 22 36
6 **ESP**
49
55 30

53 60 52
54 19
38 **Root** 39
58 41

@understandinghumandesign

© Karen Curry Parker   #QuantumHumanDesign

- Center for Self, identity, love & direction
- Magnetic Monopole resides here
- Attracts things to you that are a part of your life purpose
- Associated with the liver & blood
- 45% of the population have it Open/Undefined

WHEN IT'S OPEN/UNDEFINED

- Here to be wise about love, Self & identity
- Deeply sensitive
- Geographically need to be in the right place with the right people
- Questions their lovability
- Can pursue goals & dreams of others
- Can be indecisive & doubt own judgement
- Can take on the identity of others

Questions to ask yourself (Open/Undefined G): "Do I question my lovability? Am I struggling to find direction? Do I love where I live, where I work and who I'm with? Am I taking on other people's personalities?"

Affirmation for your Open/Undefined Identity (G) Center: "How I experience myself changes depending on who I am with. I choose to surround myself with people who feel good to me. Place is very important to me and I create an environment that soothes me. When I am in the right place, the right opportunities come to me."

· The Resource (Will) Center ·

A Defined Will Center will always be red on your chart. When you have a Defined Will Center, you have consistent access to willpower. You can be willful.

This aspect of our identity is an individuated part of our unique expression that is in service to the greater good.

The Defined Will Center is designed to work and then rest. Generally speaking, if you have an open or undefined Sacral, but your Will is defined, it is very important to take time off or go on vacation periodically; if you push too hard without rest, you may end up with heart troubles or stomach problems. *(Of course it truly depends what else you have going on in your Design.)*

If you have a Defined Will Center, you will energetically empower others by making them feel as if they can do anything. And they can, as long as they are standing in your aura.

Be gentle with others who don't seem to be able to "just do it" the way you can. The truth is that most people don't have willpower and need to enter into their commitments in a different way than you.

In the Defined Will Center you have the ability to surrender to personal self (Ego) and rise up connected to Source (Higher Self). My Will = Ego vs. Thy Will = Surrender

Also having a Defined Will, people can project promises or commitments onto you. So be careful and clear about what you do promise to the people and with the commitments you make. People will also feel like you will want to take care of them.

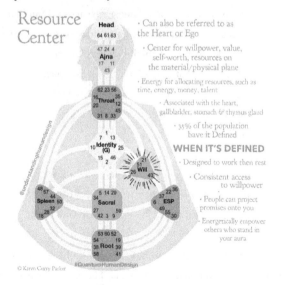

Resource Center

· Can also be referred to as the Heart or Ego

· Center for willpower, value, self-worth, resources on the material/physical plane

· Energy for allocating resources, such as time, energy, money, talent

· Associated with the heart, gallbladder, stomach & thymus gland

· 35% of the population have it Defined

WHEN IT'S DEFINED

· Designed to work then rest

· Consistent access to willpower

· People can project promises onto you

· Energetically empower others who stand in your aura

© Karen Curry Parker   #QuantumHumanDesign

Optimal expression: Potential to use Who you are in the world as a way of serving the Cosmic plan.

Shadow side: Identity can only be in Ego

Allow the natural flow of this energy to carry you rather than try and drag it in your own strength.

Affirmation for your Defined Will Center: "It's important for me to rest. Rest allows me to recharge my willpower. I honor the promises that I make. I make deliberate promises and understand that people expect me to keep my promises. I am gentle with my expectations of others. Not everyone can just do the things that I do."

When you have an Open/Undefined Will Center, it's crucial that you use your Strategy to make agreements and promises. If you don't, you'll be using energy you don't have and run the risk of entering into the wrong situations and feeling obligated to make yourself follow through. And you might miss the right opportunity, because you'll be busy forcing yourself to do something you really don't want to do.

Because the Will Center is also all about value and the material plane, it's also very common that you may have a tendency to undervalue yourself. It's common for people with Open Will Centers to undercharge for their business services or even give their services away for free.

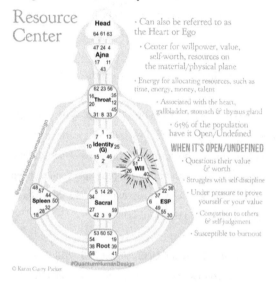

Resource Center

· Can also be referred to as the Heart or Ego

· Center for willpower, value, self-worth, resources on the material/physical plane

· Energy for allocating resources, such as time, energy, money, talent

· Associated with the heart, gallbladder, stomach & thymus gland

· 65% of the population have it Open/Undefined

WHEN IT'S OPEN/UNDEFINED

· Questions their value & worth

· Struggles with self-discipline

· Under pressure to prove yourself or your value

· Comparison to others & self-judgement

· Susceptible to burnout

© Karen Curry Parker

Remember that the Open Centers are our deepest sources of wisdom. The Open/Undefined Will Center can help you become very wise about what is truly valuable in life. You may, with time and experience, become very wise about what you are worth, both in the area of business and in your personal life. You may also become wise about knowing when it's time to work and when it's time to rest.

You might be wondering, if I don't have willpower, how will I get things done? You can and do get things done, but you have to enter into each of your commitments according to the Strategy for your Type.

When you have an Open Will Center, it's very important for you to understand that following your Strategy may save your life. We're all conditioned to believe that we have willpower. We are the "just do it" society. And, of course, if we force ourselves to "just do it" outside our Strategies, we fail and end up feeling lousy and burned out.

Questions to ask yourself (Open/Undefined Will): "Do I feel like I have something to prove? Am I questioning my worth? Am I under-valuing myself?"

Affirmation for your Open/Undefined Will: "I enter into all agreements according to my Human Design Strategy. I make promises and commitments very carefully and deliberately, and only according to my Strategy. I have nothing to prove and I value myself deeply. I fearlessly ask to be paid what I am worth."

· The Creative (Emotional Solar Plexus) Center ·

The Defined Emotional Solar Plexus will be brown on your Chart. If you're part of the 50 percent of the population that has it Defined, you carry emotional energy at all times.

The Channels connecting your Emotional Solar Plexus to other Centers will determine the kind of emotional wave(s) that you experience. Some of you may experience high emotional highs and low emotional lows, with plateaus in between. Others will have only small undulations in your emotional frequency and some may experience a slow ride up and deep plummet down and then it repeats.

Transformation
(Individual)
Wave

High Highs
& Low Lows

Channels
12/22

39/55

Sustainability Wave
(Tribal)

Small Undulations

Channels
40/37
59/6
19/49

Synergy Wave
(Collective)

Slow incline up, deep plummet & then it repeats

Channels
35/36
41/30

Because of the wavelike nature of emotional energy, it is easy to mistake the melancholy of the low end of the wave for depression. If you are emotionally defined, depression can become a big problem if you are looking for a reason why you are feeling down.

We have a lot of judgment against negative emotions in our society. But not all negative emotions are destructive. Melancholy or the low end of an emotional wave is also a very important creative energy. It allows a person to evaluate an issue from many different emotional perspectives.

If you are emotionally defined, it is a good idea to keep a log of your emotional energy on a daily basis. Each person has their own unique emotional rhythm, and knowing your emotional pattern will help you make healthy decisions and understand the timeframe that you may need in order to reach emotional clarity about a decision.

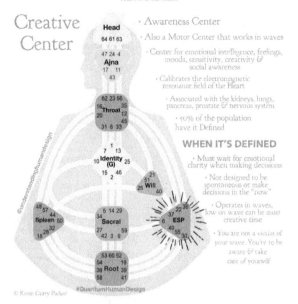

Creative Center

Head
64 61 63

47 24 4
Ajna
17 11
43

82 23 56
16 **Throat** 35
20 12
45
31 8 33

1
7 13
10 **Identity (G)** 25
15 46
2

21
51
26 **Will** 40

48 57
44
Spleen 50
41 32
28
18

5 14 29
34 **Sacral**
27 59
42 3 9

22 36
37
6 **ESP** 49
55 30

53 60 52
54 19
38 **Root** 39
58 41

· Awareness Center

· Also a Motor Center that works in waves

· Center for emotional intelligence, feelings, moods, sensitivity, creativity & social awareness

· Calibrates the electromagnetic resonance field of the Heart

· Associated with the kidneys, lungs, pancreas, prostate & nervous system

· 50% of the population have it Defined

WHEN IT'S DEFINED

· Must wait for emotional clarity when making decisions

· Not designed to be spontaneous or make decisions in the "now"

· Operates in waves, low on wave can be most creative time

· You are not a victim of your wave. You're to be aware & take care of yourself

@understandinghumandesign

© Karen Curry Parker   #QuantumHumanDesign

Because you experience emotion in waves, it is crucial that you honor your process. Emotional definition is always your Authority, so no matter what Type you are, wait until you have emotional clarity before you take action or respond. You are not Designed to be spontaneous.

Waiting for the right emotional state before taking action will keep you from leaping into emotional decisions and regretting them later.

Affirmation for your Defined Emotional Solar Plexus: "I take my time making decisions and know that I reach clarity over time. I am here to be deliberate, not spontaneous."

Fifty percent of people have an Open/Undefined Emotional Solar Plexus. Emotionally open individuals are here to learn about emotional energy and become wise about feelings.

When you are emotionally open, you are truly empathic and can take in other people's emotional energy and amplify it. This can be a great gift. Many emotionally open people are great at sales because they can instantly read their client's emotional status and tailor their sales pitch accordingly.

Because the Open/Undefined Emotional Solar Plexus will take in emotional energy and amplify it, this can be a very painful center to have open when you do not understand how it works. It is easy to think that the emotions you are experiencing are your own, and if someone else's energy is negative, it can be painful when it flows into your awareness.

Consequently, it is common for open emotional people to develop coping strategies that involve being nice, people-pleasing, avoiding conflict, or having a secret life. It is not that emotionally open people are weak or lack character. It is truly more painful for these people to enter into highly charged emotional situations.

It is crucial to become conscious of emotional energy when you are emotionally open so that you can allow that frequency of energy to flow through you without you feeling responsible for it or as if you need to fix it. Be an emotional screen, not a sponge.

Creative Center

Head
64 61 63

47 24 4
Ajna
17 11
43

62 23 56
16   35
20 **Throat** 12
45
31 8 33

7   1   13
10 **Identity (G)** 25
15   46
2

21
51 **Will**
26   40

48
57   44
Spleen 50
32
28   52
18 28

5 14 29
34
Sacral
27   59
42 3 9

22 36
37
6 **ESP**
49 55
30

53 60 52
54   19
38 **Root** 39
58   41

- Awareness Center
- Also a Motor Center that works in waves
- Center for emotional intelligence, feelings, moods, sensitivity, creativity & social awareness
- Calibrates the electromagnetic resonance field of the Heart
- Associated with the kidneys, lungs, pancreas, prostate & nervous system
- 50% of the population have it Open/Undefined

WHEN IT'S OPEN/UNDEFINED

- Can avoid sharing truth to not experience conflict
- Can be super kind or nice to a fault to not make any "waves"
- Highly empathic & here to become wise about emotional energy
- Can be impulsive & spontaneous or addicted to drama
- Can be overwhelmed by groups & confrontation can leave them unable to function or think

@understandinghumandesign

#QuantumHumanDesign

© Karen Curry Parker

Oftentimes a person who is consistently acting out with great drama is emotionally open. This person is picking up and amplifying the emotional energy of their family and friends. On their own, however, these people are actually quite mild and don't experience a lot of emotional energy.

Question to ask yourself (Open/Undefined Emotional Solar Plexus): "Am I avoiding truth and conflict and trying to keep everyone happy?"

Affirmation for your Emotional Solar Plexus: "I can make decisions in the moment. I pay attention to the source of my emotions and allow others to experience their feelings without making their experience my own. I'm very sensitive and I trust my insights about other people's feelings. I take frequent breaks when the emotional energy is too intense."

· The Divine Timing (Root) Center ·

If you have a Defined Root Center, the square at the base of your BodyGraph will be brown.

This means that you have a fixed way of processing adrenaline energy, and it will operate cyclically, depending

84

on which of the lines you have colored in around your Root Center. You will get things done when the adrenaline pulse is there; when you don't have that adrenaline pulse, things won't necessarily get done.

You have a natural cycle for your adrenaline energy and you'll have your own unique pulse.

If you have a Defined Root Center you are somewhat immune to adrenaline pressure. That doesn't mean that you don't experience stress.

However, your stress may come from other factors or through other Open Centers that you may have in your Design. Simply put, when you have a Defined Root Center, things get done when they get done.

Root Center Connections:

· **Root Center connected to Emotional Solar Plexus:** when your mood (wave) goes down or gets low then your physical energy will go down as well.

Divine Timing Center

Head
64 61 63

- Pressure Center
  - Also a Motor Center that pulses off and on
- Adrenal pressure & stress driver
- Momentum to move life forward
- Associated with the adrenal glands
  - 60% of the population have it Defined

Ajna
47 24 4
17 11
43

Throat
62 23 56
16 35
20 12
31 8 33
45

Identity (G)
1 7 13
10 25
15 46
2

Will
21
51 40
26

Spleen
48 57
44 50
32
18

Sacral
5 14 29
34
27 59
42 3 9

ESP
22 36
37
6
49 55
30

Root
53 60 52
54 19
38 39
58 41

WHEN IT'S DEFINED

- Root to ESP - when your mood (wave) goes down or gets low so does your physical energy

- Root to Sacral - you'll get things done when the formatting energies (any Channels from Root to Sacral) line up, as they operate in pulsing off & on again

- Root to Spleen - when you sense the timing is right (when it feels right) then you'll get things done

@understandinghumandesign

© Karen Curry Parker

• **Root Center connected to Spleen:** when the timing is right (it has to feel right) then you will get things done.

• **Root Center connected to your Sacral:** you will get things done when the formatting energies line up, as they operate in cycles of pulsing on and off.

Affirmation for your Defined Root: "I honor my root pulse and wait for the energy to get things done. I get more done when the energy is "on". When the energy is "off" I know that it is my time to rest and restore myself."

86

If the square at the bottom of your BodyGraph is white, then you have an Open/Undefined Root Center. It takes in adrenaline energy from others and amplifies it.

Someone with an Open/Undefined Root might enjoy the rush of being in front of a crowd or other adrenaline-charged experiences, such as skydiving or bungee jumping. More simply, they may opt for safer adrenaline fixes, such as caffeine or chocolate.

Divine
Timing
Center

· Pressure Center
  · Also a Motor Center
    that pulses off and on
· Adrenal pressure & stress driver
· Momentum to move life forward
· Associated with the adrenal glands
  · 40% of the population
    have it Open/Undefined

WHEN IT'S OPEN/UNDEFINED
  · The pressure to get
    things done so you can
    be free is amplified
    & intensified

© Karen Curry Parker

Because this is a Pressure Center people can sometimes feel that they are under pressure to be free. Meaning, people who process energy this way have a hard time relaxing or playing unless all their work is done. They will feel such pressure to get things done that they don't ever allow themselves time to recharge their batteries. Eventually, they can become so drained that they are ineffective at work.

Sometimes, the energy taken in the Open/Undefined Root Center might be too much for a person, and they may suffer from stress or a panic disorder. People can have different levels of sensitivity in their Open/Undefined Centers.

The truth of the Open/Undefined Root is that the work is never done. If you give an individual with an Open/Undefined Root a job to do, they will do it very quickly in order to get out from under the pressure of having to get it done.

Naturally, we tend to assign these people more work because the more work you give them, the more pressure they have to get it done, and the more they do. It can be a never-ending cycle. That's why it's crucial to realize that the Open/Undefined Root Center is just an energy center and you don't have to be a victim to that energy.

Question to ask yourself (Open/Undefined Root): "Am I always in a rush to get things done so I can be free of pressure?"

Affirmation for your Open/Undefined Root: "I set realistic goals. I make powerful decisions about being free and know that things will get done when they get done. I use pressure to create more energy and at the end of the day, I rest and relax even if my "to-do" list is long. I make decisions according to my HD Strategy even if I feel pressure. I breathe and relax knowing there is an abundance of time to get things done."

· The Mastery (Spleen) Center ·

The Defined Spleen Center will be brown on your BodyGraph. When you have a Defined Spleen, you're designed to be in the moment. Your sense of timing will be "right now." You will have a sense of time and consistent intuitive insights in the moment.

Defined Spleens have very powerful immune systems. Because the immune system is so strong, it's easy for a person to "miss" the first symptoms of an illness. They may not notice they are sick until they are very, very sick.

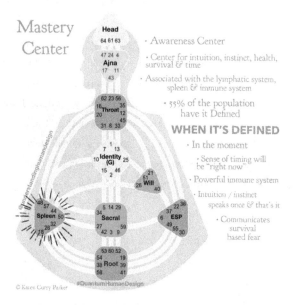

Mastery Center

Head
64 61 63
· Awareness Center

Ajna
47 24 4
17 11
43
· Center for intuition, instinct, health, survival & time

· Associated with the lymphatic system, spleen & immune system

Throat
62 23 56
16 35
20 12
45
31 8 33
· 55% of the population have it Defined

WHEN IT'S DEFINED

Identity (G)
1 13
7
10 25
15 46
2
· In the moment

Will
21
51 59
26 40
· Sense of timing will be "right now"

· Powerful immune system

Spleen
48 57 44
50
32
28
18
· Intuition / instinct speaks once & that's it

Sacral
5 14 29
34
27 59
42 3 9

ESP
22 36
37
6
49 30
55

· Communicates survival based fear

Root
53 60 52
54 19
38 39
58 41

© Karen Curry Parker   #QuantumHumanDesign

It's also common for people to keep working through an illness. It's important to remember to check in with your body periodically if you have a Defined Spleen. Sometimes other people may notice that you are sick before you do.

The intuition of the Defined Spleen speaks once and then never again. That gut feeling that you should or shouldn't be doing something is your Spleen speaking to you.

90

Because the Spleen is survival based, it can also communicate to you with fear. Some of those fears include a fear of inadequacy, a fear of the future or the unknown, a fear of the past repeating itself, a fear you're failing your responsibilities, a fear of failing or that your dreams will never be realized, a fear that life is meaningless, and a fear that nothing will ever be perfect or good enough.

It's very easy to becomes paralyzed by these fears. The challenge of the Defined Spleen is to figure out whether your intuition is giving you an important message about survival or whether you are simply experiencing the energy of the Spleen, and you need to push forward with understanding and insight.

This is where living your Strategy is so important. If you are experiencing the fears of the Spleen, use the Strategy of your Type to decide whether you should do something or not. Don't let the fears of the Spleen paralyze you into a state of inaction.

Affirmation for your Defined Spleen: "I trust my intuition. I listen to my "gut" feelings and take guided action. I listen to my body. I rest and take care of myself. I honor my sense of time. I remember that not everyone is as fast as me and I flow with Universal Timing."

An Open/Undefined Spleen means that you likely have a sensitive immune system. It may seem like you get sick easily, but what that really means is that you are very sensitive to the subtle changes in your body, and you notice when you start to feel a little "off." You may be very sensitive to medications or you may even do better with homeopathic remedies.

Mastery Center

Head
64 61 63

Ajna
47 24 4
17 11
43

· Awareness Center

· Center for intuition, instinct, health, survival & time

· Associated with the lymphatic system, spleen & immune system

Throat
62 23 56
16   35
20   12
        45
31 8 33

· 45% of the population have it Open/Undefined

WHEN IT'S OPEN/UNDEFINED

Identity (G)
1 13
7
10   25
15   46
   2

· Highly sensitive & intuitive

· Medically empathic

Will
21
51
26   40

· Can be paralyzed by fear

· Struggles with time/timing (always late or always early)

Spleen
48 57
   44
   50
18 28 32

Sacral
5 14 29
34
27   59
42 3 9

ESP
22 36
37
6
49 55
   30

Root
53 60 52
54   19
38   39
58   41

© Karen Curry Parker   #QuantumHumanDesign

When you have an Open/Undefined Spleen, it means that you don't have consistent access to "feel-good" energy. People with Open/Undefined Spleens like to be around people with Defined Spleens. It makes them feel nurtured and strong.

People with Open/Undefined Spleens can have a hard time letting go. This can include possessions, addictions, relationships—even grudges.

An Open/Undefined Center is unlimited in how it can experience the energy of a particular center. That means that you can experience unlimited intuition. It just won't always be the same. You may experience "gut feelings" one day, have "inner knowingness" on another day, and hear a guiding voice or have a prophetic dream on a different day.

Because the Spleen is also the Center for time, it's common for people with Open/Undefined Spleens to struggle with the concept of time. Many are chronically late, while others who have had bad experiences in the past with being late are compulsively early. It can be difficult for people with Open Spleens to rush.

Remember, Openness is where we carry our wisdom. When a person with an Open/Undefined Spleen begins to understand Splenic energy, they become wise about healing, intuition and time.

Question to ask yourself (Open/Undefined Spleen): "Am I holding onto things (or people, pain, etc.) for longer than I should?" "Is fear holding me back from things I want to do in my life?"

Affirmation for your Open/Undefined Spleen: "I easily let go of all things that do not serve my highest good. I honor my body and the messages it sends me. When I feel sick, I rest. I honor my own sense of timing, and respect other people's sense of time and always wear a watch. I trust my intuition and know that I receive intuitive insights in many different ways."

· The Evolution (Sacral) Center ·

If you have a Defined Sacral Center, it will be colored in red on your BodyGraph. When you have a defined Sacral, you are designed to work. The challenge is, of course, finding the right work that you love.

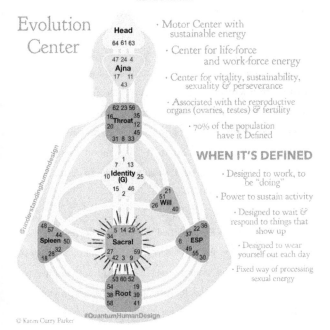

Evolution Center

Head
64 61 63

47 24 4
Ajna
17 11
43

62 23 56
16   35
Throat   12
20   45
31 8 33

1
7   13
10 Identity 25
(G)
15   46
2   21
51
26 Will 40

48 57   37 22 36
44   6 ESP
Spleen 50   49 55 30
28 32
18   5 14 29
34
Sacral
27   59
42 3 9

53 60 52
54   19
38 Root 39
58   41

@understandinghumandesign
#QuantumHumanDesign
© Karen Curry Parker

· Motor Center with
sustainable energy

· Center for life-force
and work-force energy

· Center for vitality, sustainability,
sexuality & perseverance

· Associated with the reproductive
organs (ovaries, testes) & fertility

· 70% of the population
have it Defined

WHEN IT'S DEFINED

· Designed to work, to
be "doing"

· Power to sustain activity

· Designed to wait &
respond to things that
show up

· Designed to wear
yourself out each day

· Fixed way of processing
sexual energy

A lot of people with a Defined Sacral feel frustrated because they hate their jobs and feel stuck in their work situation. This is usually because they have entered into their relationship with their work incorrectly.

The energy of the Sacral Center is counterintuitive to how most of us have been raised in this culture. Generally speaking, we have been raised to believe that we have to go out and "make things happen."

If you have a defined Sacral motor you are designed to wait for things to show up. The Sacral is all about waiting and responding to whatever shows up in your outer reality. Sacral energy works best if you learn to wait for the right thing to show up and then respond to it. Remember, though, just because it shows up doesn't mean you have to do it. You do have the freedom to choose.

Defined Sacral's are designed to wear themselves out every day. It's very important to sleep when you are exhausted. If you are waiting for your second wind, you are running on energy that you don't really have and eventually your health will suffer.

If you have a Defined Sacral and you are having a hard time falling asleep at night, that simply means you did not get enough physical activity during the day.

The real key to understanding Sacral energy is to understand that a Defined Sacral Center gives you access to sustainable life force and work force energy. This is very important to remember, because it is one of the key differences between a Sacral being and a Non-Sacral being.

Affirmation for your Defined Sacral: "I wait with grace and patience knowing that the right opportunities will show up for me. All I have to do is respond to the world and I will joyfully do the right work and be with the right people. I fearlessly honor my response and know that I am internally driven to be in the right place at the right time, doing the right work."

When you have an Open/Undefined Sacral Center, you have the ability to take in and amplify work force and life force energies for short periods of time.

This means that in short bursts, people with Open/Undefined Sacral's can work as hard as or even harder than those who have Defined Sacral's. But remember the key word in understanding the energy of the Sacral is sustainability and a person with an Open/Undefined Sacral Center cannot maintain a high level of energy for a prolonged period of time without really burning themselves out.

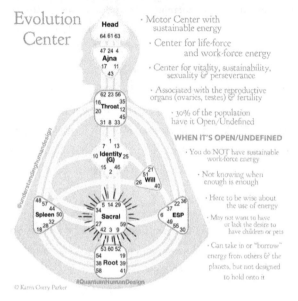

If you have an Open Sacral Center, you are not here to work a Monday-Friday, 9-to-5 job. And for most people hearing that they are not designed to work in the traditional sense is a great relief! You will probably do best finding a way to work that has some level of flexibility built into it. There are a lot of Non-Sacral people who, at around 40 years old, have literally fried their circuits.

Because sustainability is such an important factor in a Non-Sacral Being, it's important for you to always ask yourself if you are doing more than enough and to help yourself recognize when enough is enough.

Collectively, we have a lot of beliefs about the value and importance of work. A Non-Sacral Being does not have the energy for sustainable labor. Because of this, many Non-Sacral Beings get a lot of judgment from others about being lazy or incapable. But Non-Sacral Beings have their own wisdom and energy to add to the planet. They just work differently.

As a Non-Sacral person, you need alone time to discharge the excess Sacral energy from your system. Both alone time and adequate sleep are crucial for you to stay healthy.

✦ **Question to ask yourself (Open/Undefined Sacral):** "Do I know when enough is enough?"

✦ **Affirmation for your Open/Undefined Sacral:** "I am not here to work in the traditional way. I can work hard in· short bursts and then I need alone time to discharge the extra energy I carry. I recognize that my energy is mutable and I take care of myself and let go of the expectations of others. I am very powerful when I am using my energy correctly."

CHANNELS AND GATES

The 9 Centers on the BodyGraph are all connected to one another through what are called, Channels and they span all throughout the BodyGraph connecting to the nine Centers. The Channels are like your circuitry in your Design.

Each Channel has a number on either end called a Gate. There are two Gates for each Channel and a total of 64 Gates. Gates represent specific energetic themes (archetypes) in our Design as Human Beings.

There are a total of 36 Channels *(four of the Gates are used more than once in different Channels.)* Each Gate and Channel in the BodyGraph has a theme or an archetype that adds a different "flavor" to your personality and energy configuration.

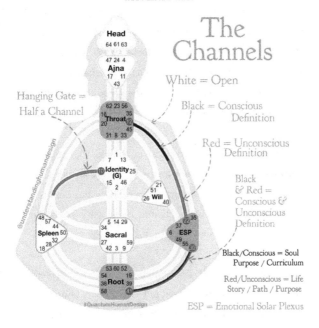

The Channels

White = Open

Black = Conscious Definition

Red = Unconscious Definition

Black & Red = Conscious & Unconscious Definition

Black/Conscious = Soul Purpose / Curriculum

Red/Unconscious = Life Story / Path / Purpose

ESP = Emotional Solar Plexus

Hanging Gate = Half a Channel

The position of the planets at the moment of our birth (and approximately three months prior to our birth) are what Defines or Activates the Gates in our Design. Our Definition in our Design are energy aspects we experience consistently. Every BodyGraph has the same 36 Channels and same 64 Gates in the same locations. The differences between Design's is what is Defined (colored in) or Undefined (open or white).

101

When both Gates are Defined/Activated it Defines the whole Channel AND the Centers at either end of the Channel. *(As you can see in this picture above, the Gates 12 & 22 are Defined along with the 41 & 30 which Defines the whole Channel 12/22 & 41/30. Therefore, defining the Throat, Emotional Solar Plexus and Root Centers.)*

When a Channel is colored in **'black'** that represents personality traits and energy aspects that we are consciously aware of and that is our Soul Purpose, what our Soul is here to experience. This is calculated using your birthdate or otherwise known as your conscious birthday.

When a Channel is colored in 'red' that represents traits and aspects that we're not consciously aware of (our unconscious definition) and also represents the Life Story or Life Path/Purpose for us in this incarnation.

The unconscious birthday is roughly three months prior to your birth and coincides with a large spurt in brain development in the cerebral cortex while a baby is in utero. It is approximately eighty-eight astrological degrees from the moment of your birth.

When a Channel is colored in 'both **black** and red' it represents both the conscious and unconscious aspects & both the Soul Purpose and Life Story.

When a Channel is 'white' it represents an Open Gate at the end of it. We will always take in energy from the planets and the people around us in our Openness and amplify it. We will always experience the energy in our Openness in variable and inconsistent ways.

When only 1 of the 2 Gates at either end of a Channel is Defined/Activated, it is called a 'Hanging Gate' (like we see in this pic above with the Gate 10.) A person with a Hanging Gate is always attracted to people who have the other half of the Channel. This is what we call electromagnetic attraction.

Each Chart has a total of 26 activations designated by the 13 planets listed on your Chart *(Kiron does not activate a Gate).* The planets position at the moment of your birth and approximately *three months prior* to birth are what activate or define the Channels and Gates in your Chart. The numbers in black and the numbers in red on either side of your BodyGraph, next to the planetary symbols, correspond with the colored in Definition on your Chart.

Planetary Symbols

@understandinghumandesign

☉	Sun
⊕	Earth
☊	North Node
☋	South Node
☽	Moon
☿	Mercury
♀	Venus
♂	Mars
♃	Jupiter
♄	Saturn
⚷	Kiron
♅	Uranus
♆	Neptune
♇	Pluto

LINES, PROFILES & THE INCARNATION CROSS

When you look at the numbers (Gates) next each planet symbol on your Chart, you will see that each Gate number has a smaller number next to it. For each Gate there are six different **"Lines"**, each line being a further expression of your uniqueness. The lines of the Gates do not show up on the BodyGraph itself and their meaning can be revealed to you during a <u>Human Design Reading.</u>

Each line has a specific expression or "personality". The position of your Gates is expressed also in lines, giving you even more insight into how that Gate will be expressed in your life. Each line has a specific energy that will influence how the Gate is expressed.

TRANSPERSONAL lines are energies that are all about experiences in relationships with others.

Hexagram

Line 6	
Line 5	— **Transpersonal**
Line 4	
Line 3	
Line 2	— **Intrapersonal**
Line 1	

INTRAPERSONAL lines are energies that are self-focused and all about personal experience and understanding.

Karen Curry Parker
@understandinghumandesign

Lines 1 through 3 in the Profiles are intrapersonal lines and are energies that are self-focused and all about personal experience and understanding.

Lines 4 through 6 in the profiles are about transpersonal energy and all about experiences in relationships with others. Some people, by design, are focused more on their own life process, and others are more oriented toward relationships.

The six lines are:

1. The Resource
2. The Responder
3. The Explorer
4. The Stabilizer
5. The Visionary Leader
6. The Adept

Line 1: The Resource

✳ Insatiably curious, investigative

✳ Needs to "understand" before they can do anything

✳ Introspective

✳ Foundational line of the lower trigram

Quantum Purpose: To lay the information foundation for the security and safety of all.

Line 2: The Responder

✳ Likes and needs to have alone time

✳ Designed to be "called out"

✳ Can be shy or coy

✳ Intrapersonal/lower trigram

Quantum Purpose: To integrate knowledge, energy and wisdom, and wait for the readiness of others to call them out.

Line 3: The Explorer

✳ Learns what works by first learning what doesn't work

✳ Here to be "experts" in what works based on experience

✳ No such things as a "mistake" or "failure" if a lesson was learned

✳ Experiential learners

✳ Intrapersonal/lower trigram

Quantum Purpose: To explore and experience possibilities and share your experiences with others to protect and serve them.

Line 4: The Stabilizer

✳ Foundation of upper trigram

✳ Transpersonal

✳ Moves from one foundation to the next

✳ Fixed

✳ Uncomfortable with limbo or uncertainty

✳ Their relationships and connections are everything to them

✳ They care deeply and are highly sensitive to judgement and criticism

Quantum Purpose: To lay the foundation of community and connection and prepare the way for sharing and spreading of ideas.

Line 5: The Visionary Leader

✳ Universalizes whatever is in their Chart

✳ "Savior" or not depending on the projection field

✳ Mysterious, seductive, compelling, persuasive

✳ Transpersonal

Quantum Purpose: To serve as a "Karmic Mirror" for others and to support the healing process through the reflection by teaching and sharing the highest potential of humanity possible.

Line 6: The Adept

✳ Tri-phasic life cycle

✳ *Phase 1 (Birth-29): Pioneer Phase-Exploring and Experimentation

✳ *Phase 2 (30-49) On the Roof: Learning/ Healing— Integration, introspection, reflection

✳ *Phase 3 (50-end of life): Kiron Return - Fully Adept— Fully embodied to share what you're here to share with the world as a role model.

✳ Can seem aloof

✳ Late bloomers

✳ Transpersonal

Quantum Purpose: To experience, integrate and demonstrate the highest potential of consciousness on the planet and to quietly show us how to live it.

There are twelve different personality **"Profiles"** in Human Design. A Profile comes from the Lines of the Gates in a Chart's conscious and unconscious Sun sign. The Sun sign is the first sign on a Chart under the **"Soul Purpose"** and "Life Story" columns, also noted as **Mind/Body** or **Personality/Design.**

The lines are the little numbers just to the right of the big numbers. They look like exponents or a number being raised "to the power of" in mathematics.

Profiles tell you about major life themes that you will encounter, and they illustrate another way in which your personality interacts with the world. Everyone comes into the world with a specific Profile and purpose. Knowing your Profile can help you see some of the themes that you will encounter as you move toward fulfilling your purpose.

The Human Design Chart

Life Story   Profile = Character you're here to play   Soul Purpose

2/4
Conscious &
Unconscious Sun
Lines = Your
Profile (Character)

There are
a total
of 12
Profiles

Line   Line

Your Profile shows you the character you're here to play in this incarnation.

Each number in a profile has a specific meaning. The first number in your profile is an element of your personality that you will be **consciously** aware of. The second number in the profile may be unconscious and more hidden from you.

The twelve Profiles are derived from the six possible lines of a particular Gate. Each of these six lines represents a different archetype or style of behavior. Your Profile can be thought of as an explanation of your conscious and unconscious archetype and the themes associated with that archetype. Most people are aware of their unconscious profile but because it is unconscious, they do not have a lot of real control over the expression of it.

The **12 Profiles** are combinations of two gate lines (the **conscious** line followed by the **unconscious** line):

· 1/3 Resource/Explorer

· 1/4 Resource/Stabilizer

· 2/4 Responder/Stabilizer

· 2/5 Responder/Visionary Leader

· 3/5 Explorer/Visionary Leader

· 3/6 Explorer/Adept

· 4/6 Stabilizer/Adept

· 4/1 Stabilizer/Resource

· 5/1 Visionary Leader/Resource

· 5/2 Visionary Leader/Responder

· 6/2 Adept/Responder

· 6/3 Adept/Explorer

The final piece of the chart that ties the whole thing together is called the **Incarnation Cross**. The Incarnation Cross is comprised of the energies that make up your conscious and unconscious Sun and Earth signs—the top four black and red numbers on your Human Design Chart.

The Human Design Chart

Incarnation Cross 35/5 | 63/64

These four energies combined comprise about 70 percent of your personality expression. The Incarnation Cross is basically the storyline a person is here to play and live out.

There are a total of 192 basic incarnations crosses, each one a reflection of the solar and earth transits and each basic cross has multiple variations for each, making up over 700 crosses. The Incarnation Cross offers us a deeper explanation for the path of a Soul and the journey of a lifetime.

Definition of the chart refers to the colored-in channels or connections between Centers.

Single Definition means all of the centers that are colored in or defined in the chart are all connected.

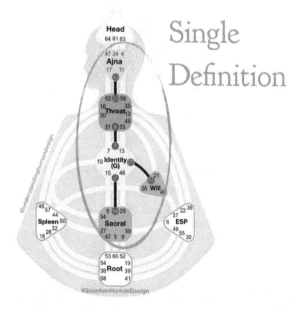

Single Definition

Split Definition means there are two distinct groups of energy centers that are connected within the group but are not connected to each other.

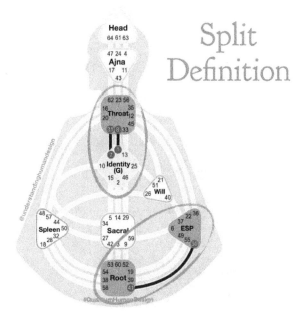

115

Triple Split Definition means there are three distinct groupings of energy centers that are independent and not connected to one another.

Quadruple Split Definition means there are four distinct groupings of energy centers that are independent and not connected to one another. Quadruple Split Definition is fairly rare.

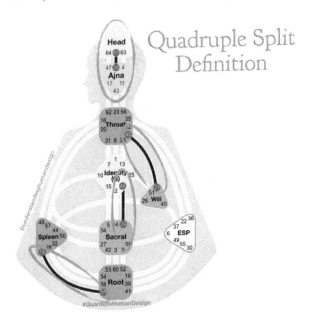

An energy split can make you feel as if you have certain very distinct aspects to your perception of yourself. For example, in this chart (see below), you may feel you have a very powerful mind and can get "lost in your head" but that you also have an "earthy" and primal part of your personality as well.

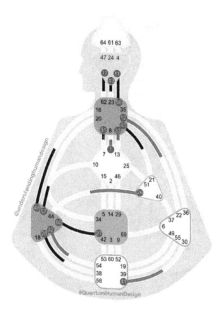

We are often attracted to partners who have the Gates that "bridge" our Defined splits. When we are with that person, we feel "whole" or that all the parts of ourselves are unified, which is indeed what happens, at least energetically.

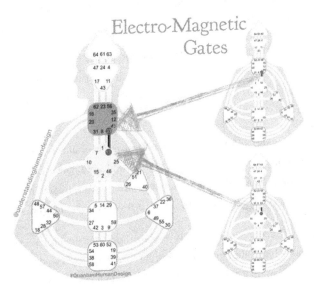

CONCLUSION

When we are born, the energy of the world begins to take us away from the Truth of Who We Really Are. Your genetic lineage, your experiences, your pain, trauma, and beliefs that you learn from the people around you, condition you away from that Truth.

The Universe is infinitely wise and kind. Despite how we might struggle and even turn away from the Truth of Who We Really Are, the Universe continues to leave us clues all along the way.

Living true to your Human Design Type allows you to interface and connect with the natural abundance of the Cosmic Plan and supports you in aligning with your destiny— the lessons you sought to master before you even incarnated.

It seems counterintuitive sometimes that living true to ourselves simply means following what feels right and good in a way that feels right and good. We do have to struggle to grow at times. Struggle is in our hard-wiring....*Suffering is not.*

We suffer when we turn away from ourselves. We suffer when we resist Who We Truly Are. Resistance to our Authentic Self is the greatest source of pain in people's lives.

You owe it to yourself to live in a way that is true to Who You Really Are.

You also owe it to the world.

Imagine for a moment that every human being on the planet represents a colorful thread that, when woven together, makes a beautiful tapestry. The tapestry is only as beautiful as the sum total of all the threads. If a thread is out of place, missing or pulled, it affects the entire face of the tapestry.

You play an important part in this world. You are so important that we would not be who we are right now without you.

At this crucial junction in time, the world needs you to take your right place—the place you intended for yourself to take before you even incarnated.

Living true to your Human Design Type and Strategy, allows you to follow the path you set out for yourself, minimize pain and resistance and, ultimately, step into the full and easy expression of Who You Truly Are.

From my Heart to yours,

Karen Curry Parker

WAYS YOU CAN STAY CONNECTED

Join the Understanding Human Design Online Community:

https://understandinghumandesign.com

Instagram:

https://www.instagram.com/understandinghumandesign/

Facebook:

https://www.facebook.com/understandinghumandesign/

Pinterest:

https://www.pinterest.com/understandinghumandesign/

YouTube:

https://www.youtube.com/understandinghumandesign

Receive a Reading:

https://www.quantumalignmentsystem.com/

human-design/find-a-human-design-specialist/

Become a Certified Quantum HD Specialist:

https://www.quantumalignmentsystem.com/human-

design/become-a-human-design-specialist/

Human Design Store:

https://www.humandesignstore.com